BUILDING A HOME–BASED BUSINESS: INSIGHTS THAT CAN HELP YOU ACHIEVE SUCCESS – PART I

Shivaram Swamy

Preface:

This ebook gives you a complete insight of the different home-based business opportunities. It also provides you a clear understanding on the different ways you can successfully build your home-based business.

This ebook is part of an ongoing series of ebooks that will be published in the future. One of the most important aspects that you need to consider when reading this ebook is to be resonant with the latest trends.

All the contents written in this ebook are original. Under no circumstances, any of this ebook can be copied or reproduced without written permission from the author.

If you liked my ebook, I would appreciate a good review on Amazon. It will be really appreciated if you can subscribe and share with your network.

TABLE OF CONTENTS

Introduction

The main goal of this e-book is to provide you a comprehensive vision of starting a successful home-based business.

In the present world, there have been a great trend in starting a home-based business. Many people come into the industry with the intent of starting a home-based business thinking it's a very lucrative profitable model, and make lots of money overnight.

The reality is- that's not true. The success rate in any home-based business is only 3%, with a failure rate of 97%. In order to achieve success, one has to clearly understand the roadmap of the strategy that works vs the strategy that doesn't. In order to do this, one needs to develop a clear understanding of different variables. These include: Market, Market Niche, Product, Traffic Sources, End Customer personas etc. Each and every detail is extremely important that nurture the success of the business.

Before exploring the different opportunities that are explained in this e-book, it is very important that we understand the 6 important stages of the customer conversion journey.

The six stages of the customer conversion journey are as below:

➢ Suspects.
➢ Prospects.
➢ First-Time Buyer.
➢ Repeat Customer.
➢ Client.
➢ Advocate.

It is very important that we build a clear roadmap in this journey. Now, we will elaborate each of the above stages that will provide us complete clarity of the process.

Suspects:

This is the first stage of the customer conversion journey. In this stage, most of the visitors scroll through the landing page and are yet to make a decision whether they want to subscribe or sign up for the product offer or newsletter. The average time that we get for us to convert the suspects to the prospects is about 3 seconds. It is also very important that the visitors who approach the landing page should be part of the targeted traffic sources.

Prospects:

Prospects are members who subscribed to the product or service. They are ready to listen to the product owner and receive the newsletters, emails etc. The prospects are also called as prospective buyers. With repeated follow-ups in regards to the product benefits, they are conditioned to try out the product that is currently being launched. In general, prospects tend to prefer a low-cost risk-free product.

First-Time Buyers:
First-Time Buyers are people who have bought the introductory product after careful analysis and thoughts. The Introductory product is low-cost and risk-free. This keeps them safer and helps them to increase their confidence in regards to the value of the product. This is the first step of the product buying cycle.

Repeat Customers:
When the first-time buyer likes the product, he/she has bought, they are likely to become a repeat customer. The repeat customers are more likely to buy more, since they have already bought the earlier product. This is the best stage for an upsells.

Client:
When a customer has bought multiple products from the product owner, they are likely to become the client of the product owner. It is very important that the business needs to increase the clientele.

Advocate:
Advocates are called the ambassadors of the brand. They actively promote the brand to their connections. Advocates helps to increase the overall brand value. This thereby, helps to improve product brand visibility.

This e-book covers the following topics as below:
➢ **Finding Successful Home-Based Business:**
In this chapter, you will learn more about the different ways of finding a successful home-based business. Finding a Successful Home-Based business plays a very important role in achieving our goals. The Internet is filled with plenty of shiny objects. Most people, who start their home-based business fall into the trap called the "Shiny Object Syndrome". This chapter will help you identify and avoid falling into the Shiny Object trap.

➢ **Top Reasons why many people fail in a home-based business:**
This chapter, will discuss some of the top reasons why many people fail in the home-based business. There are several factors that affect the success of the home-

based business. We will clearly focus the four major categories that clearly defeat the core purpose of success in the home-based business.

➢ **Affiliate Marketing:**

Affiliate Marketing is one of the biggest lucrative Industries in the home-based business. The core goal of an affiliate is to find the right product that people buy. There are lots of factors that one needs to know in the world of Affiliate Marketing. This chapter will cover all the core aspects that are relevant to the Affiliate Marketing Industry.

➢ **Ways to be Successful Affiliate Marketing program:**

Choosing a Successful Affiliate Marketing program requires a proper analysis and strategy. In this chapter, we will learn about the different ways we can follow in choosing a proper Affiliate Marketing program.

➢ **MLM/Network Marketing:**

One of the biggest business opportunities that most people get attracted to is the MLM/Network Marketing business opportunity. There are different kinds of MLM Business opportunities that promise lucrative lifestyle to the prospects. As with every business, the success or failure of the business opportunity depends on implementing effective strategies. This chapter will discuss the different ways, you can build an effective MLM/Network Marketing business.

➢ **Drop-shipping Business Opportunities:**

Dropshipping is one of the lucrative business opportunities that most people build their profits on. They sell the associated products on websites like eBay, Amazon, or their own websites. They pay the suppliers the associated costs and keep the profits to themselves. In this chapter, you will learn about the different Dropshipping Opportunities and how you can succeed in them.

➢ **Wholesaling Business Opportunities:**

In this chapter, you will be learning about the different wholesaling business opportunities. Wholesaling is also one the profitable business opportunity where people buy the goods and commodities in bulk and then sell them online. This reduces the overall sale price of the product.

➢ **Product Launch Opportunities:**

Having a successful product launch plays a very important role in your brand awareness. In this chapter, we will be discussing the different product launch strategies that will be helpful in your home-based business Industry.

➤ **Introduction to Digital Marketing:**

This chapter, will cover the basics of Digital Marketing. Digital Marketing is one the growing demand channels in today's market. Most people who market their product or service choose the different Online channels. The consumer behavior demand has dramatically changed these days. This chapter will help in understanding the basics of the consumer behavior.

Chapter 2:
Finding Successful Home-Based Business Opportunities:

The main focus of this chapter is to help you identify the different home-based business opportunities that you can explore and make decent profits.

The following is a list of profitable business opportunities that you can work from home:

> **Turning your blog into a Business:**

Blogging is by far one of the most profitable home-based business. This is not a get-rich quick scheme. Most people who work on blogging need to have a strong passion in some area of their lives. Blogs can be personal – and it should connect the end-user with great ease. As the user-engagement increases, and your blog starts to get more attention – this blogging business tends to become more profitable.

> **Earn $100K/year cleaning parking lots:**

Cleaning Parking lots in different commercial properties has recently become one of the profitable business you can imagine. You need to register with websites like Cleanlots.com to get some contracts. Once, there is an opportunity - you will be notified and you can enjoy a nice evening hobby in cleaning parking lots.

> **Sell your product online:**

You can easily sell your products online in websites like ebay, Kijiji, amazon etc. This helps you earn extra cash and reduce the unwanted inventory at your home. Another website that you can list your products is Facebook Marketplace. There is ample opportunity for you to earn money by listing your products online. You can also buy and sell products online to make decent profits as well.

> **List your place on AirBnB when you go out of town:**

This is one profitable niche that you can earn money when you are on vacation. AirBnB offers a listing service You maintain full control and need not rent to anyone whom you are not comfortable. You can also rent individual rooms in your room. This is a great opportunity to earn extra cash.

> **Driving for Uber:**

Depending on the city that you live in – you can earn upto $20/hr taking full control of your schedule. You can use your own car and when someone near you wants a ride- you get notification on your phone.

> **Freelance Writing:**

There is a huge demand for content writers in today's market. Freelance writing is a great opportunity for getting many projects. Websites like upwork, elance, freelancer etc. are great places to find opportunities for freelance writing.

> **Goodwill/Garage Sale Reseller:**

There are lots of items that can be purchased at very cheap rates from thrift stores and sold for higher prices elsewhere. This turns out to be a decent profit and you can be earning lots of money in the profits.

> **Ebay Business:**

Selling products on Ebay is a very lucrative business. There is a huge demand for selling products. It is a very crowded marketplace and there are many buyers who come to ebay looking for the different products that they want. It's a place where you can make great profit.

> **Home Inspector:**

You can be an Independent Contractor working as a Home Inspector. This requires certification. However, once you have been certified, then it is very easy to find opportunities to do home inspection. There are lots of people who are buying new houses each year. This becomes a very lucrative opportunity.

> **Real Estate Agent:**

Real Estate Agent isn't technically a home-based business. But, this opportunity gives you lots of flexibility to work from home. Being a Real-Estate agent requires training and certification. With experience, you can establish this opportunity as your own home-based business. This is also very lucrative.

> **Tutoring Students:**

Tutoring Students is another lucrative home-based business. You can teach students different subjects that you are good at. By offering help with the assignments, students get more support and guidance in their subjects.

> **Start a Christmas Light Hanging Business:**

If you aren't afraid of heights, and can handle being in the cold- then this is a great business opportunity for you. Some people earn a full-time salary just by hanging lights 2 months a year.

> **Car Mechanic:**

If you have great skills of a mechanic and can fix cars – then this business opportunity can be opened in your car garage. Many people want to have their cars fixed. This business opportunity can be a great one for you.

> **Mobile Oil Changes:**

Building off the previous idea, what if you came to your customer's home and changed their oil in their home garage. This can also be a great business opportunity.

> **Wedding Planning:**

Wedding Planning is another great lucrative business opportunity. Many weddings are taking place throughout the year. You can help both the bride and groom's family in charting out the expenses and accessories required for the marriage.

> **Medical Claims Billing:**

This Industry is one of the most common work-from-home Industries. You can find training courses online at websites like eLearners.com

> **Start a Daycare:**

You can start a Daycare from you home- if you have patience working with Children. Running a Daycare requires certification and once you get all the required certification, then it is easy to start a Daycare.

> **Handyman Service:**

If you are Handy, then there are lots of opportunities available for you to do lots of odd jobs. This is a great business opportunity. You can expand your business in the target market.

> **Lawncare:**

Lawncare and landscaping is another profitable home-based business. You can earn good money doing work on lawns. There is a huge scope for growth and development.

> **Photography:**

Photography is another great opportunity for you to earn good money. You can upload quality photos on websites like iStockPhoto, Pexels etc. and earn money when someone downloads your photo.

> **Virtual Assistant:**

Virtual Assistants are just like another secretary in another part of the world. They take care of all the important services required for your business from another location.

> ### Window Cleaning Business:
A lot of businesses and home owners want to get their windows cleaned. If you aren't afraid of heights – then business is a perfect opportunity for you.

> ### Start a Woodworking Business:
Woodworking is a great business opportunity of working from home. If you are skilled in making wooden crafts, you can build different models using wood and sell them on websites like Etsy.com, Ebay.com etc.

> ### Candle Making:
Candle Marking is another powerful home-based business. You can create a different variety of candles in different colors and sell them on websites like eBay.com, etsy.com etc.

> ### Massage Therapy:
Massage Therapy is another lucrative home-based business. There are lots of opportunities available in the local market. This opportunity helps you achieve great popularity in the local market, which creates a lot of demand.

> ### Clean Business Offices:
A lot of small businesses need their offices to be cleaned. This requires only a small investment to begin this work. You can work on this opportunity and get greater projects to clean larger offices.

> ### Senior Care Services:
More and more seniors are wanting to avoid nursing homes, in lieu of staying in their own homes. By offering, non-medical home care by assisting the elderly by their regular daily tasks – is a very and profitable business opportunity.

> ### House Cleaning:
House Cleaning is another great business opportunity that you can offer. If you have great janitorial skills, then you can start this business.

> ### Teach (English) Classes Online:

Conducting Online Training has by far grown in the current market. There is a huge demand for Online Learners – and this provides you an excellent opportunity for you to learn and grow your business.

> ➢ **Home Bakery:**

Home Bakery is another profitable business opportunity. If you have passion in making pastries, sweets, savories and other dishes – then the home bakery is an ideal business opportunity for you. There is always a huge demand for home bakery products especially restaurants, shops, events etc.

Chapter 3:

Top Reasons why many people fail in a Home-Based Business

In this chapter, we will be discussing some of the top reasons why many people fail in the home-based business.

According to today's market, the average success rate in a home-based business is **only 3%**. More than 97% people fail in the home-based business. There are several reasons why many people fail in the home-based business. However, all of them fall into **four major categories.** These are called the Demons of Defeat. The four major demons that affect our success are:

➢ **Distraction.**
➢ **Indecision.**
➢ **Doubt.**
➢ **Fear.**

Now, we will elaborate each of the above demons of defeat in greater detail.

❖ **Distraction:**

As well all know, Distraction is one of the biggest factors that affect our success. In our day to day lives, there are so many activities that are happening simultaneously. It is very difficult to keep our minds in multiple areas at the same time. However, the demon of Distraction uses three primary weapons. These include the following – <u>Time Traps, Life Crisis and a New Opportunity.</u>

Now, I will elaborate each of the above weapons and what you can do to counteract it.

S #:	Weapon	Scenario	Solution
1	Time Trap	A time trap is a situation when any insignificant activity such as browsing facebook posts, playing computer games, watching tv etc – that gives your brain a rest – begins to take over derailing you from your work.	Limit the activity to only 20 minutes. Often, a break is required to rest the brain. Set your alarm – before taking a break – so that you will be able to get back to work after your break.
2	Life Crisis	A Life Crisis is a significant issue in your	Spend only 50 minutes early in the

		life that bring your work to a grinding halt. Some examples include: Problems with your health, problems with the health of a loved one, financial crisis etc.	morning taking a small step in the work and spend the rest of the day dealing with the issue. Another effective way is to spend time in prayers – and focus on the next practical step. This way, you can break yourself from the trap of endless worries.
3	New Opportunity	As the Internet is filled with many opportunities, we fall into the trap called the Shiny Object Syndrome. There are several opportunities that make you feel that another opportunity is a lot easier than the existing one.	One way to solve this problem is to put all the interesting activities in a project pipeline. This can be evaluated at the appropriate time when it is right.

❖ **Indecision:**

The second demon of defeat that you need to overcome in order to achieve success is Indecision. Achieving any focus goal in life requires you making hundreds or thousands of decisions – whether it is big or small. This leads us into the Analysis- Paralysis trap. These decisions can be categorized into two forms. They are: Major Decisions and Minor Decisions.

The Major decisions will have significant long-term ramifications in the future. The minor decisions will have no significant long-term ramifications. The good news is, most of the decisions are minor decisions. However, we waste time looking for the right answer. In reality, there is no right or wrong answer. The best way, is to select an option listening to your gut instinct and be done with it.

The secret to making Major decisions is to use a well-defined Decision-Making process. Now, we will discuss the following steps in solving the major decision-making process.

Step 1: Define your Decision.

Step 2: Identify your Real Objective.

Step 3: Write down your Options.

<u>Step 4:</u> Explore Each Option.

<u>Step 5:</u> Do the Pros and Cons Analysis.

<u>Step 6:</u> Ask for Advice.

<u>Step 7:</u> Pray and/or Meditate on your decision.

<u>Step 8:</u> Make a Choice.

<u>Step 9:</u> Commit to your Decision.

❖ **Doubt:**

Doubt is one of the most dangerous demon that you need to overcome in the journey to your success. No matter, how further one goes in his journey to success – one situation that affects all of us is self-doubt. You will begin to question at some point, whether all the hard-work is worth the effort. Self-doubt destroys your inner belief and begin to make you feel disillusioned.

Initially, when you start any home-based business- you are super excited and start working hard towards your focus goal. This initial belief causes your enthusiasm rise high in your energy. At the initial stages, you make significant progress and are rapidly reaching towards your focus goal. However, after a period of time – your initial endeavor begins to wear off and you begin to lose your motivation and sense of belief.

As this happens, we come across different doubters who try to pull us down. They cast all their doubt bags on us. The people who make these kinds of comments are dream stealers. If we continue to accept the comments of the dream stealers, then your focus goal will never become a reality.

There is however, a solution to this problem!

You need to reignite your belief by focusing on your core focus goal. You also need to discard the doubt bags thrown by people on you. Once, your inner belief becomes stronger – then you will be able to work on making your focus goal a reality.

To reignite your inner belief, one way to do this is to create <u>a success vault</u>! <u>A success vault</u> is a display book that keeps record of all your past achievements. Some of the credentials that you can put in your success vault are: your recommendation letters, your achievement certificates, your awards. It is pretty much anything that you have achieved a significant honorary. This gives you a good feeling about your work.

When you are caught up in the Self Doubt scenario -these are the following steps that you need to implement:

<u>Step 1:</u> Find a quiet spot in a nice location.

<u>Step 2:</u> Look through your Success Vault.

<u>Step 3:</u> Draw energy from your past successes.

<u>Step 4:</u> Rekindle your Inner Desire.

Step 5: Gain new perspective.

Step 6: Get back on track.

Step 7: Find and Spend time with people who will support your vision.

❖ **Fear:**

The demon of fear uses several weapons that prevents your business to achieve success. However, it can be classified into three major categories. They are:

✓ Fear of Failure.
✓ Fear of Unknown.
✓ Fear of Criticism.

The <u>Fear of Failure</u> stems from a situation in the past, where you tried an opportunity and failed. Hence, it's safer never to try again. The main problem with this situation is, unless you set goals and risk failure – you can never achieve success. It is very important to realize that failure is not the final destination. It is rather a place you pass through on your way to achieving your success.

One should realize that failure is not the opposite of success. In fact, failure is a very important component for achieving your success. It is only through the process of trying and failing, we gain the knowledge we need to achieve success.

The <u>Fear of Unknown</u> is the situation where we imagine all the worst-case scenarios associated to the opportunity that we are focusing on. The main problem is, we gradually construct a wall of fear within our mind. This wall of fear separates you from your goal making it impossible to cross. The crucial thing to remember when faced with the fear of unknown – all the thoughts that are running in our mind are not real. There are three things you can do to conquer the fear of the Unknown.

❖ Replace the negative thoughts of what you fear to positive thoughts to what you believe.
❖ The second step to conquer the fear of the unknown is to gain additional knowledge.
❖ The third step is to take action by changing the fear of the mind to the practical reality of what you are dealing with.

The <u>Fear of Criticism</u> is the fear of what people may think and say about you. We are surrounded by many people who speak negative of your business. In order to conquer the fear of criticism, the following are the steps that you need to follow:

❖ Be selective about who you share your idea with.
❖ Get to work, make it happen and let the results speak for itself.
❖ Understand the people don't think about you nearly as much as you do.
❖ Also it is important to understand, that the criticism is not about you. It is about them.

Chapter 4:

Affiliate Marketing

In this chapter, we will be discussing the basics of Affiliate Marketing.

Affiliate Marketing is one of the biggest lucrative marketing business. There is a huge income stream in Affiliate Marketing. Affiliate Marketing is also called "Performance Marketing". There are plenty of channels which support the affiliate marketing program,

Some of these include: Clickbank, Amazon, Ebay, Commission Junction, Rauketen, Share-A-Sale. It is very important to understand how the affiliate marketing systems work.

The Affiliate Marketing Industry has four core players. These include:

- ❖ Merchant (a.k.a 'Retailer' or 'Brand').
- ❖ Network (the marketplace that contains the offer the affiliate chooses).
- ❖ Publisher (a.k.a "Affiliate").
- ❖ Customer.

The main beauty of affiliate marketing is that it is also called 'Referral Marketing'. The success or failure in affiliate marketing focuses on a multitude of different options. These include:

- ❖ Choosing a proper product.
- ❖ Creating an effective strategy.
- ❖ Identifying the effective traffic channels.
- ❖ Implementing the strategy.
- ❖ Measuring the results.
- ❖ Testing and Measuring results.
- ❖ Improvising the strategy.

One important thing to understand is that, there are different types of Affiliate Websites. Some of the different types of Affiliate Websites are:

- ❖ Search affiliates that utilize ppc to send traffic to merchant websites.
- ❖ Price Comparison websites.
- ❖ Loyalty websites categorized by rewards and incentives.
- ❖ Cause related marketing websites.
- ❖ Coupon and rebate websites that focus on sales promotions.
- ❖ Content and niche market websites.
- ❖ Personal websites.
- ❖ Shopping directories etc.

It is very important to understand that Affiliate Marketing is a very vast subject. There are lots of things that one needs to know about the Affiliate Marketing business.

Locating Affiliate Programs:

There are three primary ways to locate affiliate programs for a target website. These include:

- ❖ Affiliate program directories.
- ❖ Large Affiliate programs that provide dozens or even hundreds of advertisers.
- ❖ The target website itself (websites that offer the 'affiliate program').

Some of the questions that people ask about Affiliate Marketing are:

❖ **How do you become an Affiliate Marketer?**

Becoming an Affiliate Marketer is relatively very easy. There are lots of marketplaces that you can register for becoming an affiliate. Some of these marketplaces include: Clickbank, Amazon, Commission Junction, PayDotCom.com. These websites provide you the opportunity to register for free. Some merchants require you to have a functional website to understand about your brand. It is very important to read the TOS before signing in the Marketplace.

❖ **How much money can you make as an Affiliate Marketer?**

There is no limit in regards to earning money in Affiliate Marketing. Once, you have a proper working strategy in place – then the sky is he limit. There are a few things one should remember when creating a website. You need to include the Earnings disclaimer in your website. It is also very important not to breach your contracts with your Affiliate Merchant. You should also follow proper ethical standards when building relationship with your customers.

❖ **Which Affiliate Program is the best?**

An Affiliate product that offers a good product, relevant information that supports the requirements of the end user, and offers good value in all areas such as price, quality, relevance and information is the best program to choose.

In the next chapter, we will be discussing about the different ways we can choose a good affiliate marketing program.

Chapter 5:

Ways to be Successful Affiliate Marketing program

In this chapter, we will be discussing about the different ways we can be successful in the Affiliate Marketing program.

In order to succeed in the Affiliate Marketing program, the following are the 11 steps that you need to follow:

❖ **Step 1: Coming up with a Product Idea.**

Choosing an effective Product Idea plays a very important role in the success or failure of your business. Some of the core aspects that one needs to understand are – choosing a proper market, identifying the market niche, and then selecting the product.

The Market that we choose should be based out of our passion, our inner beliefs and the areas that we have a strong knowledge about. This will greatly help in our ability to achieve great results. One of the most important thing to note is – we must begin with the end in mind.

❖ **Step 2: Validating your Idea.**

Once, we have come up with a good product idea – it is very important that we need to validate the idea. To do this, we need to use the different keyword research tools, different market insights and understand the different personas. This will provide us clarity on understand the buyer market. It also helps us in understanding the seasonality of the product performance. Hence, validating your product idea is very important.

❖ **Step 3: Creating the Product.**

The third step we need to focus on is product creation. When doing the product creation strategy, it is very important that we understand – Market to a Product is much more valuable than Product to a Market. It is very important that we understand the pain points of the customer conversion journey. It is very important to understand that, the product that we create solves the problems that the associated customers are facing.

❖ **Step 4: Finding Affiliate Program partners.**

In the fourth step, we need to focus on finding the Affiliate Program partners. There are numerous partners out in the Internet space. Some of the major partners include: Amazon, Clickbank, CJ, Share-A-Sale, PayDotCom. This is one of the toughest part of the research – where we need to find the right audience who are interested to buy the product that you are looking to sell.

❖ **Step 5: Review the products in your niche.**

In the fifth step, it is very important to review the products in your niche. There are plenty of products that you can review. One important aspect, is to find the target market of interested audience who are looking to buy your products. It is very important to establish the relationship between the target market and the right audience.

❖ **Step 6: Shortlist the products that you want to sell.**
In this step, we begin to shortlist the products that we are looking to sell. This is done based on the results obtained in the product review. We keep the products that are selling very well and drop the low-performing products. This helps to optimize the overall product sales.

❖ **Step 7: Build the website.**
Building a website is very important for your business. Some of the typical CMS platforms are: WordPress, Magento, Shopify etc. These platforms are relatively easy to build your website. Once you have a good product website, then it is very important to build associated landing pages.

❖ **Step 8: Create associated product landing pages.**
Creating associated product landing pages is very important for your business. The main goal of a landing page is to provide the end user a valuable insight in regards to the product. The main conversion goal of a landing page is convert visitors to subscribers.

❖ **Step 9: Build your email marketing list.**
Having a strong email marketing list is very important for your business. Email Marketing plays a very important role in regards to your subscriber growth. This is very important for the business. As it is always said – "The money is in the list". We really need to have a strong responsive list for building a strong email marketing campaign.

❖ **Step 10: Educate your audience with live webinars.**
Conducting live webinars plays a very important role for the success of your business. This will help in achieving great results in your business. Webinars educate the audience more about the product, provide solutions and increase their engagement. This helps to provide great results in sales.

❖ **Step 11: Grow your business.**

Once all of the above steps are properly implemented, then growing your business becomes easy. It really helps producing massive financial results in the future.

Chapter 6:

MLM Marketing/Network Marketing

In this chapter, we will be discussing about the Network Marketing business opportunities. As the growth of the Internet, there are many Network Marketing business opportunities that are currently growing.

The main concept of a Network Marketing company is a two-fold policy. The first, is to sell the marketing product. The second, is to build the team. Every network marketing business model is different.

One of the most commonly old business opportunities that we are all familiar with – is Amway. Amway had given the breakthrough to the Network Marketing world in 1949. The company is still growing by recruiting more sponsors and selling products.

There are many MLM companies that are currently in operation. Some of them include:

- ❖ Herbalife.
- ❖ ACN.
- ❖ INCruises.
- ❖ Organo Gold.
- ❖ YTB Travel.
- ❖ Avon.

One of the biggest challenges in the Network Marketing Industry is to build the team of the right go-getters. We will now cover the top 10 tips that you need to follow, to achieve success in your MLM business.

- ❖ **Brush up on the Realities of MLMs.**
- ❖ **Find the company with the Product that you Love.**
- ❖ **Be Genuine and Ethical.**
- ❖ **Don't promote your business to your friends and family.**
- ❖ **Identify your target market.**
- ❖ **Make an Effort to Share your Product/Business Plan every day.**
- ❖ **Sponsor, Don't Recruit.**
- ❖ **Set a Goal for Parties or Presentations.**
- ❖ **Listen and sell the Solution.**
- ❖ **Learn how to Market.**
- ❖ **Stand out from other distributors.**
- ❖ **Develop a system for following up.**

Now, we will elaborate each of the above steps in greater detail. It is very important that we follow each of the above steps. This will help you achieve your profitable dream lifestyle that you are planning to pursue.

❖ **Brush up on the Realities of MLMs:**

One of the biggest realities of MLM is that- there are many pyramid schemes in the market. It is very important to stay away from the MLM scams. The first step is to understand well about the direct sales Industry as a whole, research MLM companies carefully, and determine if you are a good match with your sponsor. Although you can get rich in MLM, however your success is dependent on having strong knowledge and action.

❖ **Find a Company with a Product that you Love:**

In today's market, too many people are getting caught up with the hype of potential big income from MLM. They fail to identify the product that they are planning to promote. You can't sell something or share what you are planning to promote -unless you have a very deep interest in the product. Do your MLM research or partner with a company that has a product, which you are excited about. Don't forget to look into the company's compensation structure, before you join and make sure that it is favorable to you.

❖ **Be Genuine and Ethical:**

One major reason why many IBO's get bad reputation is – that direct selling gets bad reputation of the kind of hype that many MLM sponsors make. They share all sorts of fake success stories – and convincing them they can also be very successful in the business. Always remember this, Legitimate MLM's want you to be honest. If you love your product, your enthusiasm is enough to promote it.

❖ **Don't promote your business to your friends & family:**

It is not a good idea to promote your business to your friends & family. This can really cost your relationship. Most companies tell you to make a list of 100 people you know and convince them to join your business opportunity. This is really not the way a business should run. You need to identify your target market and then work towards it. Always, treat this business like any other business.

❖ **Identify your Target Market:**

One of the biggest mistakes that most of the MLM IBO's make is that; they choose the wrong target market. They look for everyone as a potential customer to recruit into the business. Like any other business, you need to identify your target market and promote your products to those people.

❖ **Make an Effort to Share your Product/Business Plan every day:**

Many MLM sponsors will have you focus on recruiting new business builders. It is very important for you to make every effort to share your Business Plan every day. Further, customers who love the products and services can be easily converted into business partners.

❖ **Sponsor, Don't Recruit:**
One of the benefits of MLM is the ability to bring in new business builders and profit from sales, they make in their own business. While some others use this opportunity to do the "missionary" work. This kind of strategy does not bring in any results. It only brings in more and more frustration. The focus of success is to help them with the business, not on you.

❖ **Set a Goal for Parties or Presentations:**
It is very important to understand that MLM is a person to person business. While, many people don't like that aspect in the current digital age, it is the personal touch that sells the product and business. It also retains customers and business builders. Based on your compensation plan and goals, determine how many people you need to show your products and business.

❖ **Listen and sell the Solution:**
Many companies provide you the scripts that you need to pitch in the market. One of the biggest drawbacks of this strategy is that- this does not work on any contacts. You have to qualify your contact first. Once they are qualified, then they are willing to listen to your product or service that you are looking to promote.

❖ **Learn how to Market:**
MLMers often seek a three-foot rule (everyone within 3 foot could be a prospect). It is not a good idea to build a team by talking to everyone. One must develop an effective strategy that works for the success of the business. One of the best tools that you can use to build your business is the digital technology. With this support of the Digital Technology, you have plenty of options to choose. You can determine the target market, location, demographics, interests and variety of other factors. This will help you derive the personas. This makes segmentation a lot easier. With this, you can easily learn how to market your opportunity to the right people.

❖ **Stand out from other distributors.**
One of the key aspects of success is to ensure that your strategy stands out from other distributors. It is very important to understand, that people join people they trust. To be a trusted one- you need to have achieved success in your business. The best way to achieve success is to work hard, ensuring that you have recruited the right people for your business.

A few things to remember when standing out from other distributors: 1) Don't involve in any missionary work of recruitment. 2) Use the digital technology to focus on selling the right product to the right people. 3) Identify the pain points of the people, and offer custom solutions that solve their problems. 4) Build a strong relationship with your new targeted network. 5) Convert your network into distributors.

When the above steps are followed, that way you stand out from other distributors ensuring that your business picks up speed.

❖ **Develop a system for following up:**

One of the key aspects of success is to develop an effective follow-up system. Every prospect takes time to decide, whether this business opportunity is for them. One of the best ways to create a follow-up system is email marketing. To perform effective email marketing, it is very important to choose a reliable auto-responder. Some of the best auto-responders are Aweber, Get-Response, MailChimp etc.

The second most important thing is to perform effective email scheduling so that we don't bombard the prospects with lots of promotional emails. It is very important that we nurture a long-term relationship with these prospects so that eventually they start converting into distributors.

Chapter 7:
Dropshipping Business Opportunities:

In this chapter, we will discuss about starting a Dropshipping Business Opportunity. The first and foremost thing that one needs to understand is – "What a Dropshipping Business Opportunity means". This will help in developing a clear idea about the strategy and execution of this opportunity.

What is a Dropshipping Business?

Dropshipping is one of the easiest business where the retailer (dropshipper) does not keep the inventory in hand. Instead, they transfer the customer order to the merchant. The retailer advertises the products for sale on different channels like ebay, amazon, or their own websites. Once, a prospective customer happens to order the product, then they transfer the order request to the merchant. The merchant then ships the product to the customer. The retailer pays the merchant the cost price. They then, keep the profit to themselves.

Now, we will study the key steps of running a Successful Dropshipping Business:

Some of the key steps in running a Successful Dropshipping Business are:
1. Select a Product Niche.
2. Perform Competitor Research.
3. Secure a Supplier.
4. Build your eCommerce Website.
5. Create a Customer Acquisition Plan.
6. Analyze and Optimize the Path.

We will now, elaborate each of the above steps as mentioned above. This will help in bringing complete clarity of the whole process.

❖ **Select a Product Niche:**

The success or failure of the Dropshipping business depends on the kind of product or niche that is being selected in the first place. There are several factors that needs to be taken into consideration in this regard. It is very important, to remember that product to a market is much harder than market to a product.

Some of the core aspects that you need to take into consideration, when selecting a product niche are:

> o Choose a product that gives you attractive profits: When running a Dropshipping business model, it is very important to choose a product with a good price. In general, we choose products that have good price and less costs. This helps us to get very good profits for our business.

o   <u>Low Shipping costs are very important:</u> It is very important to choose products that have the lowest shipping costs. This will help you to get more profits from the products that you sell. While searching for low shipping costs, it is also very important that – we must not compromise the overall shipping quality. Choosing reputed carriers helps a long way to ensure that the customer gets his products on time.

o   <u>Make sure that the product that you have selected appeals to impulsive buyers:</u> The product packaging, quality and delivery must be very appealing to the impulsive buyer. This helps to increase the overall sales of the product and thereby get more profits.

o   <u>Ensure that the product has a high demand and less competitive:</u> Choosing a high demand & less competitive product helps a lot in ensuring that you get a good profit margin for your product. This really helps to achieve a great opportunity for building strong relationships with your customers.

o   <u>Create your own brand:</u> Branding is a very important aspect in the Online Business. One of the biggest areas that creates a lot of revenue in the future is Brand Awareness. This ranges from choosing a company or a business name or a market niche. As the brand awareness increases, then more and more customers will prefer to buy your product.

o   <u>Sell something that isn't readily available locally:</u> When a product is readily available locally in the market, then it is less likely that your product will sell. This is extremely important – as most people go online once they know that it is not available easily in the local market. It is very important to do proper market research ensuring that a very careful selection is made before choosing the product.

❖   **Perform Competitor Research:**

Performing proper competitor research is very important for the success of the business. When starting out to the Dropshipping world, it is very important to know that you will be competing with other Dropshipping competitors as well as with other retail giants such as Walmart, Amazon, Ebay etc.

In order to do a successful competitor research, the following are the steps that you need to follow:

- o **Categorize your competitors:** Categorizing your competitors is very important and must be done at the start of the competitor research. In order to do this, you need to use different tools such as SEMRUSH, SpyFu, simple google search etc.. Do not compete with high level competitors such as Amazon, Ebay etc.

  You also need to ensure that the product that you are planning to sell is similar to the products sold by your competitors. This will help you achieve greater control on the target market.

- o **Examine your competitor's website & customer experience:** This is a very important aspect, when doing competitor analysis. We need to understand the overall customer experience with the different products and services that the customer is selling. This means, checking for the total number of reviews, product description etc. We also need to check the ease of payment for the customer. It is very important to note that the 1 star and 2 star rating gives us the best opportunity to improvise on the product performance strategy.

- o **Identify your competitor's market positioning:** In order to identify your competitor's market positioning, you need to use different tools such as SpyFu, SEMRush etc. This will provide you great insights on how the product is performing in the overall online space. Another way is to do a simple google search. This will provide you enough insights on the competitor's market positioning.

- o **Take a peek at the pricing:** A very important aspect that determines the overall success or failure of your business is pricing. Most customers look at multiple websites to check for product pricing, before they make a decision. It is very important to keep the pricing competitive enough to get the sale. The other option is to do multiple product combinations with a free product to make the offer more competitive.

- o **Analyze the customer reviews given by the competitors:** This is one of the most important steps when doing competitor analysis. When reviewing competitor products, it is very important to pay attention to the 1-star and 2-star ratings. This will give us an idea of what the customers are dissatisfied about. This provides the opportunity to improve on the product strategy. Once, we can convert every dissatisfied customer to a satisfied customer, then this helps us to increase the overall sales for our business.

o Review their performance on Social Media: One of the best tools that we can use to review competitor performance is – Social Media. Social Media helps us to analyze the overall engagement of the users in different platforms like Facebook, Twitter, Pinterest, Google+, and LinkedIn. This helps to analyze the strengths and weakness of the overall competitor performance.

❖ **Secure a Supplier**:

One of the biggest challenges in Dropshipping in securing a good supplier. There are several ways you can secure a supplier for your business. Some of the typical directories that help you to find some good suppliers are: Salehoo, AliExpress, Doba, Wholesale Direct, Dropship Direct etc.

When you select a supplier from any of the above directories, they are already filtered and screened before their business name enters the directory. However, there are a few additional steps that one needs to pay attention before finalizing the supplier they want to do business with:

o Expert Staff and Industry focus: One of the most important things that you need to consider when choosing the supplier is the expertise of the staff. When you call the supplier, and their staff has a great industry knowledge – that becomes a great starting point. The staff should be able to guide you on how to build your business effectively. They should be able to answer all questions that you ask. This is extremely important for your success.

o Dedicated support representatives: The team of the supplier should have a dedicated support which is able to offer 24/7 assistance. The support staff should be easily accessible by phone, email or chat. They should be able to resolve any issue that you have, in a breeze. It is very important that there should be no waiting time in getting hold of the support representatives.

o Invested in Technology: One of the most important things, that the suppler should have is that they need to use the latest technological tools. Their systems and strategy should be highly technology efficient. It is very important that their database should be updated and current. It is very important that there should be no discontinued, or out of stock products in the inventory.

- o <u>Organized and Efficient:</u> It is very important that the supplier should have a very organized and competent staff. They should be able to manage multiple competing priorities at the same time. Every flow of communication between the dropshipper and supplier should flow smoothly. There should be no communication gaps in the overall process. This makes, doing the business very easy and efficient.

- o <u>Takes orders via email:</u> This may be like a minor issue. But, making orders through call all the time can be very tedious and time-consuming. A great supplier would be able to take orders through email. This way, the overall efficiency of the order flow will be a lot easier.

- ❖ **Build your eCommerce Website:**

Having your own eCommerce Website is very important for your business. Building an eCommerce Website is very easy these days. There are different CMS platforms that help building your website. Some of the most popular CMS platforms that make building your website easy are: Wordpress, Magento, Shopify etc.. There are different plugins that support the eCommerce feature. These include: WooCommerce, Oberlo, etc..

The following are some of the tips in building your eCommerce Website:

- o <u>Choose your eCommerce platform:</u> Choosing a good eCommerce platform is very important for your business. One of the best eCommerce platform that you can use to build your business is Shopify. Shopify is a very robust platform that you can use to list your products. It is also secure and can accommodate multiple plugins for payment gateway and security. The other platforms that are very good are Wordpress and Magento. They are also very good eCommerce platforms to build your business.

- o <u>Pick a domain name & brand:</u> This is a very important area that builds or breaks your future in the eCommerce Online Business. Choosing a good domain name that is small, easy to remember and recognizes your product brand makes a big difference. This requires a lot of research and it is always a good idea to take guidance from different subject matter experts.

One important thing to note, Brand Awareness plays a very important role for the success of the business. Having a proper logo and tagline is extremely very important on the overall brand value of the product. These two aspects play a very important role and must be taken very seriously.

o   <u>Build your eCommerce Website:</u> Once, the platform, domain name, & product brand is chosen – then it's time to choose a proper hosting package. Some of the most common hosting companies include Hostgator, BigRock etc. For any startup company, it is best to use the Shared Hosting package.
After selecting the proper Hosting package, the we install the appropriate CMS platform. We can then build the website. Before starting to build the website, it is very important to do the appropriate product categorization and sub-categorization. This requires proper wireframe planning and strategy for SEO purposes. Based on all these parameters, we build the eCommerce website.

o   <u>Setup your merchant account:</u> Setting up the merchant account is very important for receiving payments. You need to signup with reliable payment gateway for accepting the payments. Some of the most popular payment gateways include: Paypal, Skrill, SecurePay, First Data Corporation etc. Once you have signed up with a merchant account, then it can be integrated with the website.

o   <u>Add an SSL Certificate to your website:</u> Adding SSL Certificate to your website is very important for both buyer and seller protection. This will help preventing from fraud transactions and hackers. Shopify has one of the best integration features for the SSL Certificate. It is very important to ensure that the SSL certificate is current and valid. This also helps in building trust, credibility and reputation to your buyers.

o   <u>Start selling online:</u> Once, all of the above steps are complete- then it's time to enter the market and start selling products. Some of the most common traffic sources that you can try are Google Adwords, Bing Ads, Solo Ads, SEO, Social Media etc.

You need to develop a proper Social Media strategy before you can start selling products on the different social media channels like Facebook, Twitter, Pinterest, Google+, Yotpo etc.

It is also very important to create effective landing pages, setup the Autoresponder for email marketing, and custom sales pages. Also, it is important to setup funnels in Google Analytics to analyze the customer behavior along the journey of conversion.

❖ **Create a Customer Acquisition Plan**:

Now, we will be discussing on the different strategies to create a Customer Acquisition plan. Before we get into the details of creating a Customer Acquisition plan- it is very important that we understand the customer conversion process. There are 6 stages in the customer conversion journey. These are:

✓ Suspects.
✓ Prospects.
✓ First-Time Buyer.
✓ Repeat Customer.
✓ Client.
✓ Advocate.

These stages are detailed in the Introduction chapter of this eBook. Now, we will elaborate the 8 steps of the Customer Acquisition plan. These include the following:

o Find your Users:

The first step in the Customer Acquisition plan is to find out the potential customers for your business. Once, you find out who your targeted customers are – then you should take action to seek out these people who may be interested in your products or services. There are lots of factors that one needs to consider such as segmentation, personas, buyer behavior etc.

o Figure out where your Target Customers are:

The second step of the process is to figure out where your Target Customers are. In order to do this, you need to study the product seasonality, demographics, user behavior, personas. This will provide a great deal of information, that will guide you to determine your Target Customers. This greatly helps with your overall conversions.

o Incorporate Video Content:

Videos greatly play a lot in today's conversions. Creating highly effective video content, increases user engagement and thereby improves the overall conversions. Some of the popular channels for Video Content are Youtube, Vimeo, Wistia, Daily

Motion, Viddler etc. Once, you create and upload the different videos in these different video channels- this will greatly improve the overall conversions.

- o <u>Get the Word Out:</u>

It is very important to have the word out to as many users as possible. In addition to the Online Channels, offline channels are also equally important. In order to do this, you must involve in the community engagement strategies. This means, sending out flyers at local community places, printing and pasting in notice boards, local magazines etc. This also gives an improvement in the overall boost of the product flow.

- o <u>Give away FREE Stuff:</u>

One of the best ways to improve the overall conversions is to give away the FREE incentives. People always like to try the product before they decide to buy. This helps in improving the overall engagement of the visitors and thereby turning them into buyers.

One important thing to note is that, you shouldn't give away some crappy stuff as Freebies. The product that you are giving away for FREE should be of high value to the end user. This helps to boost the overall morale of the end user thereby turning them into customers.

- o <u>Produce Quality Content regularly:</u>

Producing Quality Content regularly keeps the overall website content fresh and updated. This will help the end users come back for more. This improves the overall readership for the end user. This helps to get more returning visitors back to the website for more and more. Another important aspect that needs to be done is integrating the content with Social shares. When the end users read the content, and in order to engage the end user – it is very important to integrate the social share buttons at the bottom of the website. This makes it easy for the end-user to share the content with their network.

- o <u>Search Engine Optimization (SEO):</u>

SEO plays a very important role for the getting the business in the first page of Google. This helps in getting more organic traffic to the website. It is very important to do proper SEO for the most popular pages. This includes, writing proper meta titles, keywords, descriptions, ALT Tags etc. This helps to boost the overall conversions for your website and landing page.

   o   <u>Develop a Referral Strategy:</u>

Developing a proper Referral Strategy helps to reduce the overall marketing costs. As it is well-known – people join people they trust. One of the best ways to develop a proper referral strategy is to offer incentive referral discounts. This, helps to increase the overall flow of the returning customers for the business.

❖ **Analyze and Optimize the Path:**

Once, all of the above steps are performed – it is very important to optimize the overall path of the process flow. You need to track all the data using Google Analytics. One of the most important things to setup in Google Analytics is the conversion funnels. When you are able to track every single conversion, then you will be able to get proper insights of the overall gaps and loopholes in your conversion paths. Through the process of continuous iteration – we can minimize the overall spillage of traffic. This will help in producing great results – which eventually produces more sales to the business.

Chapter 8:
Wholesaling Business Opportunities:

In this chapter, we will discuss in detail about the Wholesaling Business Opportunities that you can possibly explore.

Once, you have achieved success in Dropshipping with different products – then it would be a great idea to start your journey as a wholesaler. Wholesaling has several great advantages over Dropshipping. This gives you complete control of the Inventory. It is very important to remember that the Wholesale trade can be supplied to consumers, commercial businesses, and other business areas.

In order to achieve success in Wholesaling, the following are some of the steps that you need to follow:

❖ **Get a proper education and training about Wholesaling.**
❖ **Decide what you want to sell.**
❖ **Determine if the business is going to be profitable or not.**
❖ **Complete all the required credentials such as Business Licensing, Business Account, Tax Identification Number etc.**
❖ **Arrange for Funding from the appropriate sources.**
❖ **Get a Warehouse and all the necessary tools required.**

Now, we will elaborate each of the above steps to develop a complete clarity of the overall process flow.

❖ **Get a proper education and training about Wholesaling:**

Getting a proper education about Wholesaling is very important. There are several courses online that offer training about Wholesaling. You must also get proper knowledge about accounting and business administration as well. This is extremely important to understand, that there are lots of aspects that you need to know about Wholesaling.

❖ **Decide what you want to sell:**

Deciding what you want to sell is a very important step for your business. One of the best ways to determine, what you want to sell is to dropship different product niches. This will give you the idea and confidence of the different products that people are looking to buy.

One important thing to note is that, you get in touch with many suppliers that you are interacting with. This will give you the confidence and guidance to identify those products that are selling well in the market. With this knowledge, you will be able to determine which products you need to wholesale for your business.

❖ **Determine if the business is going to be profitable or not:**

In order to determine, whether the business is going to be profitable or not, it is very important that you need to contact the manufacturers to learn the exact manufacturing costs of the product commodity. You also need to learn about the shipping costs of the product. These total costs will help you estimate your overall expense in getting the product.

In addition to this, you also need to determine the overall warehouse and stocking costs. You also need to add the marketing costs as well. On the top of these costs, you need to add your profit margin. This overall cost should go at par with your competitor pricing. With these factors above, you can determine whether this business that you have selected is profitable or not.

❖ **Complete all the required credentials such as Business Licensing, Business Account, Tax Identification Number etc.**

As a business owner, it is very important to complete all the required credentials for your business. These include: Tax Identification Number, Opening Business Accounts, and other pre-requisites required for your business. It is extremely crucial to have all the required documents ensuring that there are no issues with the legality.

❖ **Arrange for Funding from the appropriate sources.**

It is very important to arrange for funding from the appropriate sources for your business. You must be aware that, you will not be making any profits for the first 3 months. In order to survive in the business for the first 3 months, it is very important that you must have enough funding with you from reliable sources to carry on the operations.

❖ **Get a Warehouse and all the necessary tools required.**

It is very important that you need enough storage space to hold the inventory. For a startup business, it is always best to start from your garage. As the business grows, then it can be moved to bigger spaces. This way, you can make the wholesaling business very operational.

Chapter 9:
Product Launch Opportunities

In this chapter, we will discuss about the different Product Launch Opportunities. This opportunity is for innovative people who want to make a huge breakthrough in their business.

In order to succeed in any Product Launch, the following are the 8 steps that you need to follow:

❖ **Be Strategic.**

- ❖ **Go Overboard with Outreach.**
- ❖ **Know your Audience.**
- ❖ **Target Major Media Outlets.**
- ❖ **Build your superfans.**
- ❖ **Bring Brand Ambassadors into your Business Family.**
- ❖ **Use Pre-Launch videos to drive leads.**
- ❖ **Technology is your friend.**

Now let's begin from the basics...

What is a Product Launch?

A product launch is a launch when a company or a business decides to launch a new product to the market. It can either be an existing product or an innovative product, which the company has ever made. This requires advanced knowledge of the product strategy, innovative ideas and vision and accurately targeting the buyer needs.

What is the main purpose of a Product Launch?

The primary purpose of a Product Launch is mainly business growth. Product Launches build base and helps in bringing in new customers to the market. This is really the core aspect that helps to grow the business to greater heights. It also improvises brand awareness and recognition.

Now, we will elaborate each of the above steps mentioned above:

- ❖ **Be Strategic:**

In the start of the product launch, it is very important to be strategic. Having an effective strategy plays a very important role in the success or failure of your product launch. You need to think of your business from the customer's point of view. It is very important to understand their pain points and ensure that your product effectively addresses their pain points. There are two aspects in creating a product strategy. 1) You can create an effective strategy for an existing product. 2) Or, you can define a new product strategy for a new innovative product.

Once, the roadmap is clear – then it is very easy to choose the appropriate channels of conversion for the product launch.

- ❖ **Go Overboard with Outreach:**

It is very important to remember that, "Obscurity kills businesses". If you don't go overboard, you won't get attention needed to be successful. It is always very important to go the extra mile to achieve the results that you desire.

❖ **Know your Audience:**

One of the most important aspects that determine your success is to understand your audience personas. We need to identify the buyer audience based on the market insights, behavior, demographics and other important relevant data points. It is also very important that you know about your product value. Once, you are aware of your product value, then it is easy to target the right audience to deliver the product.

❖ **Target Major Media Outlets:**

You need to target the major media outlets during your product launch promotion. Some of the typical media outlets include: Facebook PPC, Bing Ads, Google Adwords, Youtube, Native Ads etc. It is very important to ensure that your audience gets the message at the right time. This helps in increasing the overall brand awareness of your product launch.

❖ **Build your superfans:**

One important thing to remember is that, it is not a good idea to jump into the product launch without first building a community of superfans. You need a high degree of super-targeted subscribers who are interested in receiving your product newsletters and other offers. This engagement drives more enthusiasm for your subscribers. They then, start getting more enthusiastic in receiving your newsletters and then eventually start buying your products.

❖ **Bring Brand Ambassadors into your Business Family:**

It takes a village to get buzz for your business. Building brand ambassadors is very important in building your business family. Product Ambassadors actively promote your product or brand to their associates. This helps to bring in more business for your product launch. One of the most important thing that you need to remember is, Ambassadors are members who are "all-in", in regards to the product promotion. They are actively engaged in all the on-going activities of your business activities.

❖ **Use Pre-Launch videos to drive leads:**

One of the most important things that you need to remember is – you should use a prelaunch video to drive leads for your business. The video should be short and should not be more than 30 seconds. You use a landing page and signup form to capture the leads for your business. The email campaign offers special incentives for your subscribers to become on-going customers.

❖ **Technology is your friend:**

In your business, you should use technology as your friend. Webinars are perfect in spreading your message, in an attractive, engaging form. With the latest advent of technology – you can easily automate several of the process. This helps in making the work a lot easier. It is also very important to stay abreast of the latest aspects of the technology. This will easily help in ensuring that you are not outdated with your product launch strategies.

Chapter 10:
Introduction to Digital Marketing

In this chapter, we will discuss the basics of Digital Marketing. The core objective of this chapter is to give you the fundamental concepts of the different aspects of Digital Marketing. This will give you the confidence to gain more insights about the Online Landscape in the upcoming series of eBooks.

What is Digital Marketing?

Digital Marketing is that branch of marketing, that combines technology with marketing. Before, the growth of the technology – marketing was pretty much done offline through print media, newspapers, flyers, billboards, television etc. Unfortunately, these channels could not be measured for effective conversions.

With the growth of the Internet Technology, these problems are greatly solved. There are several online channels such as facebook, twitter, bing ads, google adwords, google organic searches etc. which provide accurate tracking of the overall buyer data. With the combination of technology and strategy, we can achieve great results in a limited period of time.

In this chapter, we will only be covering about the use of Digital Marketing technology in a very limited scope and how it will be useful for your home-based business.

Every home-based business owner has a big dream of achieving success in his business. The most important aspect that one needs to consider when starting his/her business is to understand the connection between the buyer behavior and the product that they are trying to sell.

Core Components in Digital Marketing:

Digital Marketing has several components that are extremely important in the business. Some of the core components in Digital Marketing include the following:

- ❖ **Search Engine Optimization (SEO).**
- ❖ **Pay-Per-Click Marketing.**
- ❖ **Landing Page Optimization.**
- ❖ **Email Marketing.**
- ❖ **Video Marketing.**
- ❖ **Mobile Marketing.**
- ❖ **Solo Ads.**
- ❖ **Native Ads.**
- ❖ **Google Analytics & Tag Management.**
- ❖ **Content Marketing.**

Now, we will elaborate each of the above components. This will provide enough insights on using the different aspects of Digital Marketing.

❖ **Search Engine Optimization (SEO):**

Search Engine Optimization (SEO) is one of the biggest aspects that most businesses prefer. The main goal of SEO is to be on the first page of Google for any organic searches. It all begins from doing proper keyword search. In order to do effective keyword search, you can use different keyword tools like Google Keyword Planner, Bing Ads Intelligence tools, Ubersuggest etc.

This will help you in determining the keywords that have the maximum number searches etc. Once, you determine the keywords that have high traffic, low competition, high relevance and good commerciality – then it is easy to develop an effective SEO strategy for your business.

❖ **Pay-Per-Click Marketing (PPC):**

Pay-per-Click Marketing is one of the best methods of measuring targeted traffic to your business. Some of the most common PPC channels are: Google Adwords, Bing Ads, Facebook PPC etc. One of the best features of the PPC campaign is – you control the overall ad spend, and other important metrics required for PPC. This helps in achieving the desired financial target with ease.

If you get a thorough knowledge of PPC, then it will really help you build your business. Some of the most common metrics that you need to be aware of in PPC are: Click-Through Rate (CTR), Conversion Rate, Quality Score, Exact, Phrase, Broad and Negative Keywords. These metrics will really help you understand about the core aspects of PPC.

❖ **Landing Page Optimization:**

One of the most important concepts that play a very important role for your business is Landing Page Optimization. Landing Pages play a very important role in regards to user engagement.

The main components of a good landing page are: 1) A Catchy Headline. 2) Benefits of the Offer. 3) Call to Action. These three components should be well done – so that it can yield maximum conversions for the campaign. It is very important to have multiple landing pages. We can then connect these landing pages to the rotator for maximum optimization.

The landing pages need to be rotated for effective A/B split testing. Another important aspect that needs to be performed is- Multivariate Testing. Multivariate Testing plays a very important role for moving the landing page elements to analyze the user behavior. There should be enough content in the landing page that prompts the user to input their information.

❖ **Email Marketing:**

One of the most important aspects that plays a huge role in the success or failure of your business is- Email Marketing. As it is commonly said, the money is in the list. When we build a list of very targeted subscribers -this helps to get more sales in the future.

In general, it is recommended to have at least 30 super-targeted subscribers every day. This really helps in achieving maximum conversions for your business. The most important thing that one needs to understand is- the email series should be written in such a way, that you educate the subscriber. There has to be a proper sequencing in writing the emails. This helps in achieving maximum conversion rates for your business.

❖ Video Marketing:

The main goal of Video Marketing is to promote the brand or product through videos. Some of the most popular channels in creating videos for your business are: Youtube, Vimeo, Viddler, DailyMotion etc.

In the present world, the maximum user engagement is through the use of Videos. Having a strong content strategy for videos helps in increasing the number of subscribers. Hence, having an effective video strategy is very important for your business.

❖ Mobile Marketing:

Mobile Marketing plays a very important role in product promotion. The number of Mobile users has dramatically increased these days. This gives a huge opportunity to target the mobile users. Some of the typical platforms that help with the mobile applications are: Admob, Mopub, InMobi, Startup.net etc. These mobile ad networks help to direct targeted users to the products or services that are currently under promotion.

It is very important to have highly responsive landing pages that are mobile-friendly. The user should not have any problem in accessing content through their media devices such as iPad, iPods, iPhones, Laptops, Android Devices. There has to be perfect congruence on what the user wants to what is being delivered.

❖ Solo Ads:

Solo Ads play a very effective role in marketing products. One of the best aspects of Solo Ads is – that you are renting another's email list. This really helps to get maximum conversions for your business. One of the best sites to get solo ads is udimi.com. There are several Solo Ads sellers who provide high quality service.

One of the most important thing that you need to remember in choosing a Solo Ads vendor is – they need to have high quality ratings. We should ensure that they have very good feedback and many of the people who bought their solos are happy with their services.

❖ **Native Ads:**

Native Advertising is the form of paid advertising that match the look, feel and function of the of the media format in which they appear. Native Ads are often found in social media feeds or as recommended web content. Some of the typical native ads networks are: Outbrain, RevContent, Taboola, Gemini, AdNow.

❖ **Google Analytics & Tag Management:**

Google Analytics & Tag Management plays a very important role in the measurement of the business performance. Some of the core aspects of Google Analytics is to measure the overall performance of the website health. Tag Management accurately tracks the individual user behavior in the landing page – such as button clicks, text links etc. This helps in optimizing and achieving effective targets for your business.

❖ **Content Marketing:**

Content Marketing plays a very important role for the success of your business. There are different forms of Content Marketing. These include: Documents, Videos, Podcasts, Audios etc.

It is commonly said, "Content is the King" and "Context is the Queen". It is very important that we need to achieve success by having effective end user content. This really helps in achieving the expected success in business and life.

Conclusion:

The main goal of this eBook was to provide you enough insights on the different aspects of a home-based business. Starting a home-based business can be both an exciting and challenging idea.

In the next ebook series I will be elaborating more about the different aspects of Digital Marketing and how it will help in successfully building your business.

If you liked my ebook, a positive feedback review will be greatly appreciated! This will help me keep motivated to add more ebook series in the future.

www.ingramcontent.com/pod-product-compliance
Lightning Source LLC
Chambersburg PA
CBHW030539220526
45463CB00007B/2897